God's Positive And Negative Equation

By Michael A. Danforth

Acknowledgments

Cover graphic Image used by permission. All rights reserved.
1236789 www.Fotolio.com

ISBN 978-0-9815944-4-6
September 2011

Printed in the United States of America

God's Positive and Negative Equation

Images:

Myweightliftingprograms.com
Allposters.com
Bayswater.ca
Paralegalhell.com
Mentalxpress.wordpress.com
Collincreek.org

Michael A. Danforth
Mountain Top International
P.O. Box 43, Yakima, Washington, 98907
www.mticenter.com

Editing by Arlene Baldwin
Ell Supervisor West Valley School District 363

TABLE OF CONTENTS

THE TYGER

By William Blake

"When the stars threw down their spears,
And watered heaven with their tears,
Did he smile his work to see?
Did he who made the Lamb make thee?
Tyger Tyger, burning bright
In the forests of the night,
What immortal hand or eye
dare frame thy fearful symmetry?"

(lines 17-24)

INTRODUCTION

This brief excerpt from William Blake's poem, "Tyger," is an analogy of a positive and a negative force at work in the earth. The Tyger symbolizes man; the fearful symmetry, sin; and the lamb is God. For centuries, many have wondered if God is really God; why does He allow a spiritual entity known as satan to contradict His kingdom on earth.

Why did God give satan permission to buffet Job, right up to the point of Job's own destruction? Why did God entertain a being that is dark and cynical, whose intentions are 100% evil? What does light have to do with darkness? Why does He tolerate something that is continually trying to undermine His plans and desires toward those He loves? Could it be that somewhere beneath all these questions, lies a simple answer to the good and evil equation that exists in the earth today?

In (Job 1:2, 2:3), satan was able to persuade God to give him access to Job, based on Job's loyalty to God. How is it that some evil being has the ability to persuade God to do anything, let alone have access to someone like Job, who was a model of God's character throughout the earth?

These actions from both sides lead us to believe that the evil nature of satan somehow plays a vital role in revealing or testing the true character and nature of humanity, especially God's elect.

Since the beginning of time, the relationship between God and man continues to unfold its many mysteries. Apparently, God is very interested in our motives for our devotion to Him, and satan seems to be the primary candidate for revealing those intentions.

Undoubtedly, God hates everything about satan. He hates his life, his works, even his seed.

However, it seems that if you and I are going to be tested, satan and his motley crew are the ones to do it.

Over the centuries, humanity has moved from one covenant with God to another.

Finally, through the resurrection power of Jesus Christ, God's people were reinstated with a final and everlasting covenant. Through this reinstatement, we were given the keys to claim victory over all the works of the enemy.
(Luke 10:19)

We were brought into the realization of sonship as priests and kings in the kingdom of God.

We discovered that God was no longer just our creator, but our Father. Now, our first calling is to:

"Love the Lord God with all our heart, soul, mind, and strength." The second is "to love our neighbor as ourselves." (Matthew 22:27-40)

Oh, I know, some neighbors are easier to love than others are. Nevertheless, those harder ones, those that are on the more challenging side of the equation, have a way of inviting us to reveal the true character and nature of God in us.

It seems to serve the purpose of God to tear down what the enemy has built up. This enhances one of our primary goals in life, which is to influence the kingdoms of this world for the kingdom of God.

It seems now, that while God could have eliminated his archenemy either before or after the garden event, He has chosen not to. Instead, God has given us a legal premise to destroy the works of the enemy and keep his evil intentions in check. The origin of satan has long been debated.

Though I have spent a number of hours over the years searching out such matters, my intention for this writing is not to discuss the origin of satan, but to merely evaluate why evil has always been a part of God's equation even before the world began.

While some things concerning good and evil might still be a bit vague, one thing is for certain, (the serpent) satan, otherwise known as the devil, plays a very vital, yet negative role in God's equation for all of creation.

The mystery of this negative and positive force reaches as far back as pre-creation. This mysterious equation of plus and minus, positive and negative, is woven through the very fabric of life. Some have suggested that life was completely positive prior to sin entering into the garden, but scriptures reveal otherwise.

Before the creation of man, there was a garden and in that garden stood a tree bearing knowledge of ***good and evil.*** In that garden God's glory was fully resident, as well as, a serpent more cunning than any other beast in the field. (Gen 3:1)

God's Positive And Negative Equation

There is, and has always been, a positive and negative equation at work in the earth. It is part of the poetic structure of God's kingdom. In fact, I believe it is the poetic thread of all creation. There are no materials known to man that do not have some kind of positive and negative force working within them; be it metals, woods, plastics or any other natural or synthetic material. Nothing could exist without the working of a positive and negative action; a bird could not fly, nor could fish live in the sea. None of creation could exist as they do today without positive and negative forces.

It has been said by the scientific world that the universe, as we understand it, is made of 99% dark mass and 1% light. I know that dark mass is another subject of great debate; however, the fact remains, both light and dark exist. To whatever degree, all the planets, galaxies, stars, sun, and moon make up a very small percentage of the entire known universe. None of which could ever exist without this ongoing equation of plus and minus.

The underlying foundation of physics is based on plus and minus. Physics is the branch of science concerned with the nature and properties of matter and energy. The subject matter of physics, distinguished from that of chemistry and biology, includes mechanics, heat, light, radiation, sound, vibrations, frequencies, electricity, magnetism, and the structure of atoms. All of these and more are what define the working of our universe today.

It takes the opposite of one thing to reveal the nature of another. Without false, the value of truth could not be understood, at least not to the extent that it was meant to.

Paul writes,

"For there must also be factions among you, that those who are approved may be recognized among you." (1Cor. 11:19)

Factions are defined as heresies or disunions. It implies situations where the powers of choice are in conflict with one another. Paul is simply stating that it takes false and true to reveal those who are in God and those who are not.

It takes a night to reveal the value of a day. How can cold be fully understood without the presence of heat by which to measure it? No peace without war, no joy without sadness, no love without hate, no hell without heaven and so goes this poetic thread weaving itself throughout creation.

I am not saying that love could not exist without hate or life without death; however, I believe the depth, height, width, and breadth of that love and life could not be realized to the degree that it was intended, without these two forces at work. This equation is the foundation for line upon line and precept upon precept.

Regardless of what form, before Adam or after, none could be possible without the ingredients of plus and minus. Mathematically speaking, the greater number has no value without the lesser. Therefore, we could say that the value of 100 would not be realized without the lesser value of fifty. The lower number compared to the larger enables us to realize its true worth.

It is one thing to know we are created in the image of God and it is quite another to realize just what that really means.

The positive and negative forces that are present in the earth today enable us to go from a mere image of God into the likeness of God.

These positive and negative forces are at work above, on, and beneath the earth. They are necessary in order for the knowledge of God to be realized. I hope that in these writings you discover that the opposing forces you face daily in your life are vital to the knowledge of God being revealed in you. I am convinced that the glory and power of the prophetic and apostolic spirit of Jesus Christ could not be grasped without opposing forces working in the earth. However, let me be clear, I do not believe in a declining church but an increasing one.

The glory of God is not fading, but is ever growing, becoming brighter and brighter throughout the world.

Nor am I implying that sickness and disease are given to us by God to make us a better person. In my opinion, that is just stupid thinking, no matter how you slice it. Of course, the result can reveal something glorious and wonderful in God, but it does not mean that God has to be the initiator of our trouble.

Every situation that is viewed from a righteous perspective can aide us toward a continual transformation of heart and mind. I am fully confident in the completed work of Jesus Christ toward us. The very nature of this understanding is part of the renewing process of life. Again, the fact remains; there are still no real successes or victories without obstacles or hurdles to overcome.

As I just mentioned, this writing is not one of doom and gloom, for it is a far cry from that fearful pit of despair that so often motivates people to want to run and hide until Jesus comes. No, this is a message of hope and courage. It is a wakeup call to those who are still looking for an easier path that leads to their intended purpose and destiny in God.

It's the revelation of the bitter and the sweet, and how both will lead us into a maturated mind. It took the life of Jesus in the face of death for his resurrection power to be revealed. Therefore, it will take the life of the church in the face of opposing forces for the glory of God to become visible in her.

Again, I am not suggesting that we are to embrace opposition, regardless of the form in which it may come.

Nor am I implying that we go around looking for trouble in hopes of somehow proving our loyalty to God. However, we are called to embrace life in the face of death, knowing that the Creator of all life is always acting on our behalf. Just seeking Him and living in obedience to His word provokes enough trouble.

I believe the majority of our opposition lies largely within our own hearts and minds. Our ability to see into the kingdom of God is dependent upon a spiritual transformation that must take place within our own thinking.

As this occurs, we are able to rise up into a greater authority, into a sphere of righteous understanding that God has made available for all who believe in Him.

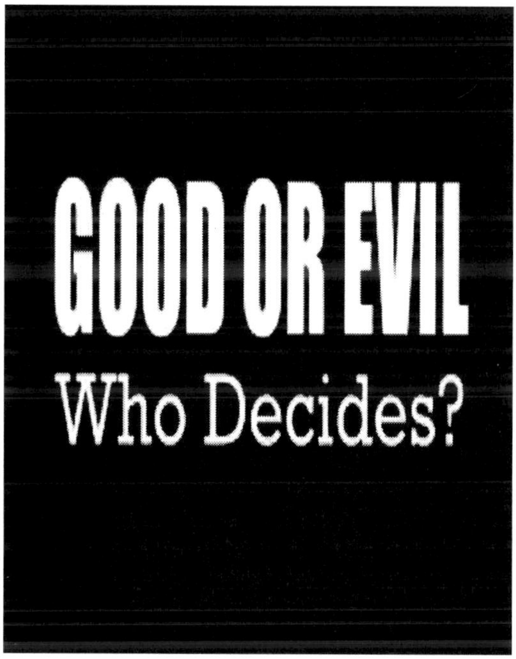

Positive And Negative Encounters

Habakkuk, the prophet, saw the knowledge of the glory of the Lord covering the earth as the waters cover the sea. (Heb 2:11)

The glory of God is continually covering the earth. A positive and negative motion plays a key role for this glory to cover the earth. I know that our tendency is to always wait for certain things in life to get better before we make our move toward our destined goal, but it's time we stop waiting for troubles to go away before we get the victory .

Lay hold of your victory now and you will see your troubles fade beneath your trust and confidence in God's glorious intentions toward you.

I'm reminded of an encounter that I wrote about in my previous book, "Last Days Desire." I have since discussed this in other writings, but I feel it is appropriate to mention it again.

We were having tent meetings in a park during the summer of 1994. One night during one of the meetings, a man stood at the main entrance of the tent with a strange looking pouch hanging over his shoulder. At first, he just stood there, staring me down, refusing to take his eyes off me. After about five minutes into my message, he started toward me, with a cold daring look full of hateful intentions. He came and stood directly in front of me, nose-to-nose; eye-to-eye.

The next thing I felt was his stinky saliva on my face, followed by his hand cuffing me upside the head. Everybody in the audience just froze, waiting for my response. My initial thought was, "How did this man get past the anointing?" So much for my spiritual theology, this meant nothing to this man.

Moments later, after realizing nobody was too concerned about rescuing me, a boldness came over me, or maybe it was just a brave desperation. Whatever it was, it caused me to grab his head and pull it toward my face saying, "You foul spirit, I rebuke you!" Yikes! To my great surprise, it seemed to be working, because all of a sudden the arm

that held the pouch went limp, letting the mysterious canvas bag fall to the floor. I then heard a rumbling sound coming from the bottom of his stomach working its way up to his throat. He let out a loud growl as he dropped to the ground, pulling me down with him. As soon as his knees touched the matted grass beneath our feet, a few courageous people became unfrozen and latched on to his arms and waist. Moreover, as if his efforts were not enough, he tried to bite my neck like a gruesome vampire determined not to give up without one last meal.

Then most unexpectedly, right in the middle of all this intrusive action, I heard the Lord say, "Michael, I want to move now!" I thought, "Now?" "Yes, now!" I looked around until I spotted my wife, Lori and I said, "Lori! God wants to move now!" She said, "Now?" "Yes," I replied, "now!" I quickly jumped out of the chaotic huddle and said, "Take that man out of here! God wants to move now!"

The next thing I knew, there were two or three other young men who had been sitting on a picnic table approximately twenty yards outside the tent. They came running toward me as if they had been shot out of a slingshot. As they entered the tent and got within a few feet of where I was standing, they threw their hands up in the air, and shouted, "We want this Jesus!" as they fell backwards to the ground.

This was the final fuse that caused an unprecedented move of God to sweep over the entire tent and park that night, heralding the victory of the Lord over all the works of the enemy. I later found out that the pouch he was carrying contained a large bowie knife that was sticking about three quarters of an inch out of the front of it. His intention had been to ram me with the knife, so he could be promoted to a higher seat in an occult group that he was a member of.

No, I did not like having my life threatened, nor did I appreciate being hit or spit at. But I would gladly stand in the face of all that opposition again just to see the glory of God made visible in the lives of all those who were there that night. It is true, light really does shine in the darkness. (John 1:5)

Hot And Cold

"I know your works, that you are neither cold nor hot. I could wish you were cold or hot. So then, because you are lukewarm, and neither cold nor hot, I will vomit you out of My mouth." (Revelation 3:15-16)

To say that you are lukewarm implies that you are trying to live outside of the two very powerful forces, which were specifically designed to reveal the function and nature of God's presence and glory in the earth. Being lukewarm means that you are living in the realm of complacency, where very little positive or negative fruit is being produced. Both must be in order for the plans and purposes of God to be realized.

It takes the good in light of the bad for us to see just how wonderful good really is. A glass of water is just a glass of water, until it is offered to you on a summer day registering 110 degrees Fahrenheit. Though the water itself has not changed, its value becomes much greater under less desirable conditions.

"As cold water is to a weary soul, so is good news from a far country." Proverbs 25:25

Such is the love of God. His love is unchanging, yet seemingly more realized in the midst of extreme darkness. We can never really know what hot is without the evidence of cold. The existence of the two has the power to reveal a heart that is lukewarm toward the things of God. The realm between hot and cold is where lukewarm Christianity is produced, and thus detestable in the eyes of God.

It was the cold heart of Pharaoh that revealed the fire of God's purpose in Moses. This stark contrast caused Israel to stand up and embrace their deliverance. The coldness of Pharaoh's heart was just as important in revealing the power of God as was the tender heart of Moses.

"For the Scripture says to the Pharaoh, for this very purpose I have raised you up, that I may show My power in you, and that My name may be declared in all the earth." Rom 9:17

Since the beginning of time, God has made it very clear that His intentions are to make Himself known.

In light of these intentions, He has made it just as clear, that He will have mercy and compassion on whomever He chooses. I believe the elections of God are based upon an insatiable desire to reveal His love, glory, and power throughout the entire world. (Rom 9:18)

In the winter of 1996, we got a considerable amount of snow in Yakima, Washington. For the most part, we were unprepared for the volume of snow that fell that winter. We generally get a little snow every year, but over all, it never seems to stick around very long.

However, this was one of those years when it snowed so much, that the city could not keep the roads plowed; schools were closed; and roofs were caving in because of too much weight. Power outages were making it difficult for people to keep their houses warm, which led to frozen pipes. It seemed to be the longest winter ever. I will never forget the conversations of many as we came to the end of that most unpleasant winter.

Oh, the thought of spring! How we longed for the warmth of spring! No more snow, ice, or slushy roads. No more tension from driving, wondering if our kids would drive sensibly enough to keep their cars on the road. Spring! Green grass and flowers! Lord, give us sunshine. The same sun we had complained about the summer before was now, the most inviting thought in our minds. How could we have ever grumbled about something so wonderful, so glorious, as the sun?

It is amazing how one thing in light of another introduces a completely new field of understanding and appreciation. So often in life, we do not appreciate the simplest things, either because of too much exposure, or because of the lack thereof. The negative impact of one thing caused us to realize the real value of another.

What meaning does good news really have without the contrast of bad? The good news is, Jesus Christ offered himself as a living sacrifice and rose victoriously that you and I might be saved from a sentence of death. The bad news is, without the redemption power of Jesus Christ working in our lives, death, and eternal separation are certain.

GOOD NEWS, BAD NEWS

Positive And Negative Trees

It took two trees to reveal the plan and purpose of God. Even though one was forbidden while the other was not, it took both trees for the plan and purpose of God to be fulfilled in the earth. It took the ugliness of one to reveal the true beauty of the other. Why would God create a garden with such wonder and beauty and right in the middle of all that tranquility plant something that had the potential of causing total destruction? Obviously, the tree of knowledge of good and evil was serving a purpose in the midst of all that had been created without ever being consumed by humanity.

I find it very interesting that everything in the garden revolved around two trees; the tree of life, and the tree of knowledge of good and evil.

Don't believe for a second that it was put there for temptation, for the Bible says,

"Let no one say when he is tempted, I am tempted by God, for God cannot be tempted by evil, nor does He Himself tempt anyone." (James 1:13)

Yet, here is a tree that carries the knowledge of not only good, but evil as well. One thing is for certain, this tree, like all the other trees, was going to play a key role in manifesting the glory God throughout the earth.

It is my belief that humankind would have eventually been allowed to eat of the tree of the knowledge of good and evil. However, they took hold of something before their time. It is obvious by their latter actions that they did not have the capacity to walk in this kind of knowledge.

I believe we were destined to be so much like God that this, unperceived knowing of good and evil, would have, in due time, become a part of our spiritual perception. Some have argued that man was already like God. I agree man was already like God concerning so much of His splendor and glory, but the Bible clearly reveals that Adam and Eve were not like God in respect to knowing good and evil.

Then the LORD God said,

"Behold, the man has become like one of Us, to know good and evil. Now, lest he put out his hand and take also of the tree of life, and eat, and live forever."

"Therefore, the Lord God sent him out of the Garden of Eden to till the ground from which he was taken. So He drove out the man; and He placed cherubim at the east of the Garden of Eden, and a flaming sword which turned every way, to guard the way to the tree of life." (Gen 3:22-24)

Having the ability to know good and evil means you have the power to judge. As soon as humanity gained this newfound knowledge, they looked upon their nakedness and were ashamed, though this was not how God viewed their nakedness. Their judgment of themselves was flawed. It is important to note they gained a knowing of good and evil, not just evil; which means, they did not fully see things the way God saw them.

Prior to this increase of knowledge, in their eyes, their nakedness was neither good nor bad, it just was. In other words, their perception of the creation of God was from a partial objective. It takes knowing good and evil in order to favor one thing over the other. Though the two are opposite from each other, it still takes one in light of the other to prefer one to the other.

The serpent was in the garden at the beginning. His intentions were to bring the first man and woman into the revelation of good and evil through the act of disobedience, thereby creating a venue for his seed to enter into the earth.

The introduction of this new world order would soon unleash its negative impact within the heart of man and thus seemingly alter the intended equation of God for all humanity. When man sinned, he veered off the mark which means he missed the goal that was intended for him, before the offense was committed. Prior to the sin nature entering into the world, God said,

"Be fruitful and multiply; fill the earth and subdue it; have dominion over the fish of the sea, over the birds of the air, and over every living thing that moves on the earth." (Gen 1:28)

One of the primary reasons for this particular order was so the knowledge of the glory of God would spread widely throughout the earth. Therefore, satan was determined to advance his sphere of influence through the vessel of man to produce his own seed. Man was destined to become the house and expression of God, not the house and expression of satan.

The Bible clearly states that demonic spirits are more apt to reach their fullest potential in having dominion in the earth through their ability to possess man rather than beast. (Mark 5:5-13).

Whenever they are forced outside of human occupancy, their efforts are less fruitful (dry places) and no rest is given to their demonic state until they can find someone to possess or influence. (Luke 11:24).

It was man's spiritual perception from the beginning that offered him/her the platform to have dominion in the earth.

Therefore, it's the battle over man's perception that satan has been fighting for since the beginning of time.
One of the greatest strongholds of the enemy is blinding minds from seeing their true state in God.

For the Bible declares,

"The god of this age has blinded the minds of those who do not believe, lest the light of the gospel of Jesus, who is the image of God, should shine on them." 2Cor. 4:4

Through the disobedience of one man, sin entered into the world, thus attempting to war against the progressive nature of God's glory increasing on the earth. (Rom 5:12)

I use the word "progressive" because the glory of God has become progressively visible throughout the history of human existence. Though at times it might have appeared bleak, His glory and purpose, have not slacked toward its final destination.

Regardless of the opposition that you might be facing in your life today, you must realize it's not there to defeat you, but for you to defeat it. Oh yes, I know, this sounds like "yuck" but as yucky as it can be at times, it's one of the primary keys to our maturity. However, this is **not** to make you think, no pain, no gain. Even though trials and tests can make us stronger, in the end, they are not the instrument of our strength, Jesus is.

Supernatural Peace

In the early 1990's I was, building homes and preaching the gospel in my spare time. During this period in my life, I started having severe focal seizures behind my left knee. They eventually diagnosed me as having a growth or cyst on the frontal lobe of my brain. Before and after I had the growth removed, the seizures were fierce. I was literally tormented day in and day out, never knowing when the seizures would hit me. When they did, it felt like a sharp knife jabbing me a thousand times over.

The pain was much worse than anything I had ever encountered before in my life. Given the history of my younger years, that is really saying a lot.

I had always pushed life to the limit. Broken ankles, legs, arms, wrists, hands, shoulders, facial bones, which Included a shattered jaw and crushed cheekbones, were just a few symptoms of my reckless ways.

(I know what it feels like to fall 40 feet to the ground and walk away with a few minor breaks. I have driven off 90-foot cliffs, smashed into cement walls and large trees. I have laid a skill saw into my leg, cutting down just short of the femur. I have shot myself with a nail gun right through the joint of my knee with a 16-penny nail.) Bicycles, cars, motorbikes, and snowmobiles were all instruments of near death experiences for me. (I could go on, but I think you get the point.)

Now, this particular pain from a growth in my brain seemed to outweigh all my previous injuries. Doctors believed the growth was the result of the numerous concussions I had received from prior accidents. Whatever the case, I felt like I had reached my limit for unwanted misery.

However, in the mix of it all, something unusual happened to me. One night I was crying out to God asking Him to take the pain away. The seizures behind my knee became so intense that the muscles and tendons in my leg would visibly pulsate, as if some unseen hand was trying to pull them out of my leg.

In that moment, I heard what sounded like an audible voice, "Michael, step out of the pain. Michael, step out of the pain now!" I thought, "What? Step out of the pain? What does that mean?"

I immediately went back into agony. Then I heard the voice again. "Michael, step out of the pain." Suddenly, an unusual peace came over me. Even though the tendons and muscles in my leg were visibly protruding underneath my skin, I felt no pain. It was as if my mind disengaged from what was going on in my body and I just stepped out of the pain.

In that same moment, an unusual courage rose up in my spirit. I knew I had heard the voice of the Lord. During one of the most agonizing moments of my life, I found supernatural peace. I found something in God that was beyond any human comprehension.

The next day I went to see a doctor who wanted to put me on more medication. I just looked at him, smiled and said, "Thanks, but no thanks", and walked out of the office. As Lori and I got into the car and drove away, I looked at her and said, "I am done. This is over. I am not taking any more medications that keep me from thinking straight. This ends now."

That was that. My life was on a new course. There have been a couple of times over the years when it tried to creep back in, but I quickly recalled the peace and faith of the Spirit, and it was gone. Mind you, I have since learned to treat my body much better, more nutritionally right, which has played a key role in me walking in continual health.

I share all of this with you so that you will know that in the face of great adversity there is peace, a peace that surpasses all human understanding.

In one of my most trying hours, I discovered a realm I did not even know existed, at least not to the degree that I had experienced until that time in my life. If you can somehow relate to any of the fear and pain I just described to you, I want you to know, that same peace, that glorious peace of God is available to you right now. Just ask Him now and He will deliver you from every fear.

"Peace I leave with you, My peace I give to you; not as the world gives do I give to you. Let not your heart be troubled, neither let it be afraid." (John 14:27-28)

Jesus Was Not An Alternative

Contrary to a lot of teaching, Jesus was not an alternative. God did not look at Adam and Eve and say, Now that you have sinned, I am going to have to come up with a better plan to get you out of this mess. No, according to the Bible, we were destined to become adopted sons through Jesus Christ, before the foundation of the world.

"Blessed be the God and Father of our Lord Jesus Christ, who has blessed us with every spiritual blessing in the heavenly places in Christ. Just as He chose us in Him before the foundation of the world, that we should be holy and without blame before Him in love having predestined us to adoption as sons by Jesus Christ to Himself, according to the good pleasure of His will." Eph 1-5.

God did not create us thinking that we would be disobedient. He created us with a hope and desire that we would live in obedience to His word for the purpose of sustaining continual fellowship and communion with Him.

God knew satan's deceptive nature from the beginning and was well aware that the enemy had the potential to pursue man in hopes of gaining control of what God had given to him. I believe the greater surprise was humanity giving in so easily and quickly.

Nonetheless, Jesus was always the "A" part of God's plan before the earth was formed. Jesus was not God's epiphany for cleaning up a terrible mess. We were destined before the foundations of the world to be holy and blameless through the Word, which was in the beginning, which was with God, which was God, which became the Son of God. (John 1:1-15)

God was very capable of creating a being that would never consider being disobedient. However, this was not the case, because through the power of choice the redemptive power of God would unleash a revelation of God's love, throughout the whole world.

Point being, either way God wins! One way or another, His love would be made known. We were created out of the spirit of perfect love and have always been destined to become a revelation of that same love. God chose to make us in light of making the right choice rather than the wrong one.

Therefore, God subjects Himself to disappointment. One of the many unique characteristics of the nature of God is that though we have the potential to act contrary to His purpose, He chooses to see us otherwise. He chooses to see the best in us, not the worst. Many philosophers over the years have been troubled with certain scriptures that appear to suggest that God creates some vessels for honor and others for dishonor.

"Does not the potter have power over the clay, from the same lump to make one vessel for honor and another for dishonor?" Rom 9:21

There can only be one reason for a statement like this, glory. I must say it again, "God is in the business of revealing His glory on earth as it is in heaven."

From the beginning, God intended for the evilness of satan and the weaknesses of man to reveal His glorious redemptive power throughout all eternity. As perfect as man was, his weakness was being vulnerable to the incitement of desire, thus deception.

However, what would appear at first to be a complete disaster, would in the end, reveal the greatest act of love, mercy and compassion ever witnessed before in all creation. Not only would humanity be forever united with God, but also the magnitude of God's love and glory would be greater realized in the end than in the beginning.

It is one thing to be loved, and it is quite another to know the magnitude of that love. (Eph.3:14-19).

Satan thought he had changed the course of God's primary intentions toward man, but in all reality, God used the negative forces of darkness to reveal the greater totality of His redemptive nature in the earth.

There is a saying that has come down through the ages. "Sometimes you don't realize what you had until you lose it."

Of course, there are some flaws in that statement, but the truth of the matter is, many people do not discover the real value of what they had, until the day they find it missing. I wonder what Adam and Eve were thinking when their eyes were opened for the first time to a realm of knowledge they never had before. I wonder how many times they rehearsed their actions, hoping they had made the right choice.

But then again, they never knew what it was to make a wrong choice in the eyes of God. Some have thought that humanity was destined to fall from the beginning, since there seemed to be no real safeguard to keep them from sinning. However, the truth is, humanity had the same safeguard in the garden as we have today. It is called, "**obedience to God's word**."

Outside of being obedient to the word of the Lord, "Do not eat of that tree," the ability to evaluate the consequences would have been impossible. They had no knowledge of acting contrary to the word of the Lord. There were no previous examples of making the wrong choice.

Nonetheless, their former perspective in God was now gone. For the first time they had come face to face with the negative force working in the earth.

A new dimension was unveiled to them concerning their own value and their beautiful oasis called, the *Garden of Eden*.

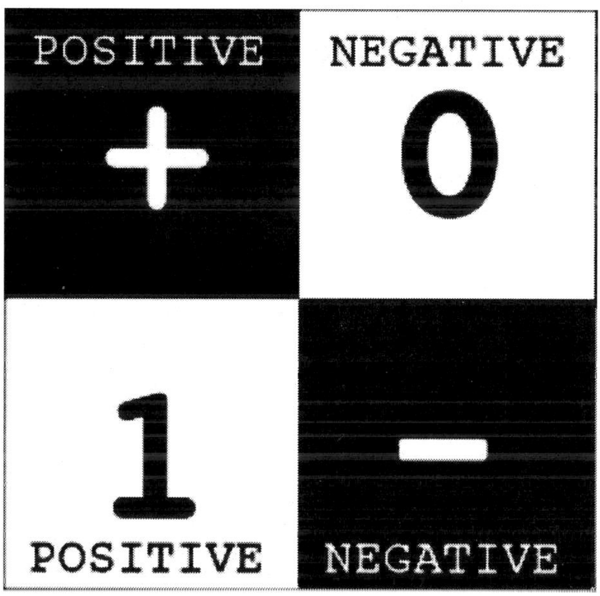

This ability to self-evaluate quickly decreased their own self- worth, though God's love toward them had never changed. It's important to note that God did not love them any less after their disobedience than He did while they were still without fault. He did not turn His back on them because of their disobedience. Of course, there were consequences to their actions, but His love for them remained the same.

However, the eventual working of sin in their lives would slowly shield their understanding of God's true nature. The nature of sin would remind them daily of their shortcomings.

Law Of Realization

"What shall we say then? Is the law sin? Certainly not! On the contrary, I would not have known sin except through the law. For I would not have known covetousness unless the law had said, You shall not covet. But sin, taking opportunity by the commandment, produced in me all manner of evil desire. For apart from the law sin was dead." (Rom 7:7-8)

I have always found these two scriptures quite insightful. Especially in verse 8 where Paul states, "Apart from the law, sin was dead." In other words, even though humanity was deteriorating from their sinful nature, the degree of evil working in them was not fully realized.

They could not understand just how bad their moral condition really was, for apart from the law, there was no way to measure the depth of their condition. Therefore, it appears the first thing on God's agenda was to bring them into the realm of realizing their true state.

I want to stop here for a moment and say that I believe this is where we now stand as a church. We are on the threshold of entering into a greater realization of our present condition in Jesus Christ. The body of Christ is being awakened to the love and glory of God.

Many of our spiritual senses, numbed by the cultures of humanity, are being made alive again to the culture of heaven. More importantly, we are getting beyond just the basics of needing God. We are going beyond survival mode and are moving into a passionate longing and desire to love God and experience Him in ways unimaginable.

Paul makes it clear that the penalty of sin (*negative force*) was not made known until it came along side the law (*positive force*).

Though the sin nature of humanity was causing man to rapidly deteriorate, the consequences of that deterioration were not clearly understood until they were exposed to the word of God in the form of the law. However, because this positive force revealed the negative working in our lives, we no longer saw the law as a good thing, but a bad thing, simply because it revealed our true state.

I am one of those people who find the discovery channel to be a very educational experience. The nature of the beast can be most amazing. Yet, it is always hard for me to watch the larger predators of the wild feast upon the smaller weaker prey, especially the young. They seem so innocent of their surroundings, unaware that they are about to become the next meal for some hungry beast.

Yet, as awful as it is, these gruesome acts of survival are a part of God's equation to keep nature balanced, at least for now. What at first appears to be a very negative action is actually, in the end, producing something very positive.

These animal instincts are currently part of God's design to keep the animal population intact. Of course, in the future that is subject to change. (that is for another book)

For the most part, it seems that the meat eaters will prey on the plant eaters, which serves as a safe guard to keeping many regions in the earth from becoming desolate of plant life altogether.

I know the pictures of the Garden of Eden look very peaceful with all the animals, birds, and reptiles at the feet of Adam and Eve and rightfully so. I believe that the Word makes it clear that there were no instinctive fears toward humanity prior to the sin nature entering into the world.

There is certainly no doubt that after the moral decline of man the force of nature took on an entirely different look. Since then, their instinctive nature has served to create a balance in the animal kingdom.

I know there are many negative things in life that appear, in the moment, meaningless. Yet, the overall results can later prove to be very fruitful.

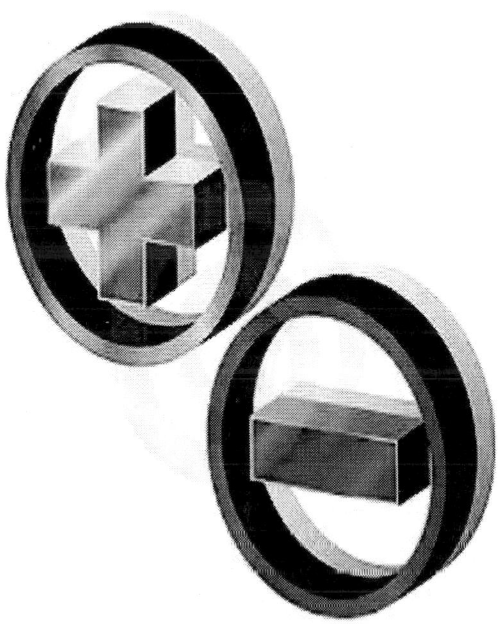

Truth And Disunity

In reference to the positive and negative equation of God, Paul writes:

"And we know that all things work together for good to those who love God, to those who are the called according to His purpose." (Romans 8:28)

I know how easy it for some to jump on the wagon of despair concerning present conditions in the world and even the church. However, I believe the opposite side of one thing reveals the positive side of another. I am not saying everything that is cruel in the world is part of God's plan for the greater good; that would be foolish thinking. However, those who trust in God in the face of cruelty are given the opportunity to see God work on their behalf. If you haven't noticed by now, convenient Christianity is over.

It is not convenient to come together as a body of believers to worship God.

It is not convenient for you to pray and seek knowledge of the Lord. It is not convenient for us to advance the kingdom of God in the earth. Therefore, we need to stop trying to work God into the corner of our own personal conveniences.

It will never happen. We do not fit God into our plans, He fits us into His. We have a purpose in life because He gave us purpose. There are powers and principalities out there that have one mission in mind and that is to deceive the world into believing that God is just an extra bonus in life. God is not an extra bonus; God is the essence of life itself. God is Spirit. God is breath; He is the air we breathe.

I am amazed at how many people today avoid the body of Christ because of previous hurts they have experienced in the church. As painful as those times might have been, it is time to get over it and get on with the plans of God for your life. I do not know anybody that has not experienced some disappointment in one form or another through divisions or heresies in the church.

Listen to what Paul has to say about the ugliness of divisions and factions within the body.

"For first of all, when you come together as a church, I hear that there are divisions among you, and in part, I believe it. For there must also factions among you, that those who are approved may be recognized among you." (1Cor11:18-19)

The word, factions, comes from the Greek word, **hairesis**, which is where we get the English word, heresies. Heresy is the distributor of disunion, division, and sectarianism. This is an ugly spirit in the church.

In short, Paul is saying, the presence of evil is really revealing what is good. In other words, in the end, these differences are going to manifest the approval of God on your life.

In other words, God is saying, 'The enemy brought this opposition in your midst to destroy you, but I am going to use it to show the world who is living in Me and who is not.'

Wow! This is amazing to me. What looked like a bad thing is going to end up in perfect order. There has been much division in the church, and there will continue to be much more in the days to come.
However, this is a time to rejoice and be strong, certainly not about disunion and division, but
about the perfect order of God that is going to emerge from its ashes.

The opposition that is coming against the bride of Christ will in the end, reveal her true beauty. I find it quite remarkable how many wrinkles can be removed, simply through the application of a little heat. Chaos always has a way of inviting the order of God in. God is into His reality, not our reality. His reality is the only thing that is real; everything else is a mere illusion.

Most people are taught that reality is in the eye of the beholder. They say, "However you see it, then that's reality to you." Yet, the truth is, there is only one view that is real, and that is God's view.

His view reaches beyond time and space. His view is eternal. Reality outside the scope of eternity is not reality at all. Only the things that carry eternal worth will, in the end, sum up our total existence.

"While we do not look at the things which are seen, but at the things which are not seen. For the things which are seen are temporary, but the things which are not seen are eternal." (2Cor 4:18)

For decades, much of church leadership has tried to protect the people from the negatives of everyday life. Yet, the value of our true position in God cannot be realized without it. This is not to imply that we do not protect those we love, yet trying to shield them from every hurtful predicament, will in the end, only make them weak.

Weakness And Strength

"Three times, I pleaded with the Lord to take it away from me. But he said to me, "My grace is sufficient for you, for my power is made perfect in weakness." Therefore, I will boast all the more gladly about my weaknesses, so that Christ's power may rest on me. That is why, for Christ's sake, I delight in weaknesses, in insults, in hardships, in persecutions, in difficulties. For when I am weak, then I am strong." (2Cor12:7-10)

Who thinks like this? Who lives with this kind of mind? Who goes around delighting in weaknesses, insults, hardships, persecutions, and difficulties? During the course of Paul's journey on earth, he discovered something very profound, *"the opposition against my life invites the power of God to rest upon me."* Now this is more than just lip service. These are face-to-face encounters that demand that the grace of God show up in your life, or you are (finished) toast.

Not only do the weaknesses in our life invite the power of God in, but His power is made perfect in us. In other words, the negative (yuck) of life can reveal a perfect work of God in us.

How many of you (reading this) have had the wonderful experience of someone saying to you, "I just want you to know how much I love you and that I am with you all the way," only to find out later that in the face of great opposition, they were some of the first to turn against you?

Relationships that have not been tested with fire are not true relationships. It takes time, trials and testing to really know who your true friends are. Any friendship short of a proving process is vulnerable to great disappointment. Paul knew what this was like. Jesus knew what this was like. Many of our ancestors of faith knew what it was like to have someone abandon them in their most needful hour. Yet they did not allow the disappointments to become their focus, because the love and power of God working in them revealed the nature of God's kingdom to those around them.

We need to stop making covenants with people we do not even know just for the sake of advancing our career or ministry. It does not matter how anointed someone is, you cannot be certain that it is a true covenant until your journey has gone through the fire.

Only relationships that have endured the positive and negative forces of life have the power to manifest the kingdom of God in the earth. There was no doubt in Peter's mind that he would follow Jesus, even unto death. However, Peter quickly realized what true devotion was all about. Jesus knew Peter loved Him, but He also knew that the enemy was waiting to sift Peter like wheat to see if his declaration of love would line up with the courage to lay down his own life.

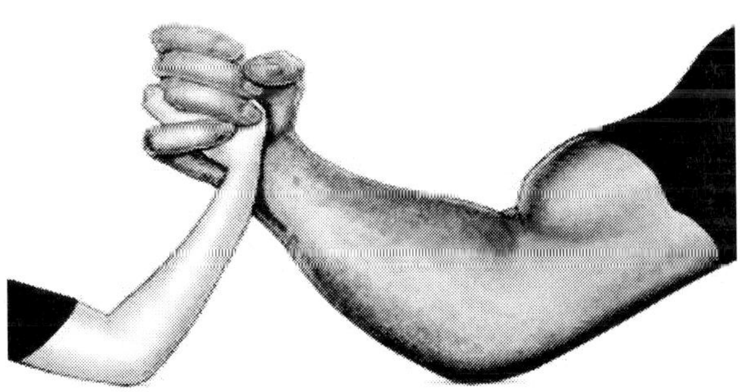

Positive And Negative Forces

"My brethren, count it all joy when you fall into various trials, knowing that the testing of your faith produces patience, but let patience have its perfect work, that you may be perfect and complete, lacking nothing." (James 1:2-4)

I have heard many speak about their faith in God, and yet, when I listen, I hear them speaking of a faith that has never been tried or tested. Faith that is not tested is not really faith at all. In these passages of scripture, James makes one thing clear, only tried faith can produce the perfected work of the Spirit. Faith that has stood in the face of trials and tests has the power to lead us into the completed work of Jesus Christ. This positive faith working on the inside of us can only reach its full potential as it is subjected to the negative forces around us. To the degree that the patience of God in us is exposed to the plus and minuses of life, is the degree that we will walk in the perfection and completeness of God, lacking nothing.

This does not mean that you might not have some unwanted issues in your life, but it does mean, in the spirit, you will lack for nothing.

It was the desert of Moses, the enemies of Joshua, the Goliath and Saul of David, the pits and despair of Daniel and Joseph, which made them our examples of endurance today.

The Hebrew children in the fiery furnace offer us a greater awareness of God's divine intervention in the face of grave adversity. There are many fears in the church today because of a "play it safe, avoid all opposition" mentality. We go to great lengths to circumvent our trials of destiny. As a result, we do not know the reality of God's supernatural intervention in our lives, as well as those around us. However, this is rapidly changing. A new generation has emerged. They will not love their lives unto death. They have exchanged their need for fame, for the love, glory, and power of God. Their greatest motivation is for the love and resurrection power of Jesus Christ to be revealed in them. Fear is not a part of their thinking.

Opposition to them spells opportunity to stand in the rest and peace of God as He moves mightily on their behalf.

Resistance Training

"And lest I should be exalted above measure by the abundance of the revelations, a thorn in the flesh was given to me, a messenger of Satan to buffet me, lest I be exalted above measure. Concerning this thing, I pleaded with the Lord three times that it might depart from me. He said to me, My grace is sufficient for you, for My strength is made perfect in weakness. Therefore, most gladly I will rather boast in my infirmities, that the power of Christ may rest upon me. Therefore, I take pleasure in infirmities, in reproaches, in needs, in persecutions, in distresses, for Christ's sake. For when I am weak, then I am strong." (2Cor 12:7-10)

It is very apparent in these few scriptures that Paul has discovered a profound revelation concerning the negative forces in life.

On one hand, they reveal his weaknesses, but on the other, they invite the power of God to manifest in his weakest hour. Some would call this resistance training. Resistance training is defined as "a form of strength training in which each effort is performed against a specific opposing force generated by resistance." (Web's Dictionary-Merriam Webster Online) Imagine something resisting your pull, push, or lift, resulting in the strengthening of your muscles.

This simple analogy depicts the natural and spiritual forces at work in the earth. The continual push and pull between earth, moon and sun, play a key role in keeping everything in its proper orbit.

There are actually two sides to spiritual resistance. On one side, you are the initial force that is creating the resistance, and on the other side, the enemy is creating resistance against you.

James writes:

"Therefore, submit to God. Resist the devil and he will flee from you." (James 4:7)

Here we find that our submission to a positive (God) enables us to resist a negative (devil). The result of submitting to the positive and resisting the negative is that the negative opposition against your life is forced to flee.

While this appears to be a very simple process, without submission and resistance, the devil will be less inclined to flee from the presence of God in you.

Once the spiritual disciplines in our life are developed to a point of maturity, the power of resistance is greatly altered. No longer is our mindset one of always having to defend our position, but we now advance to an offensive mind that keeps the enemy on the run simply because of our state of being.

Therefore, "In Him we live, move, and have our being." (Acts 17:28)

Luke quotes Jesus as saying,

"I will give you a mouth and wisdom which all your adversaries will not be able to contradict or resist." (Luke 21:15-16)

Imagine a life where the opposing forces that try to work against us, are no longer able to contradict or resist the wisdom of God in our lives. This type of life is not some imaginary way of living. In the future, you will see men and women rise up in every kingdom of the world exhibiting a profound wisdom in God. We will witness governmental leaders confounding the wise. Educators will teach with astounding insight. People all across the world will soon realize that the depth of Christianity has taken on a new contour of wisdom and understanding.

Resistance will no longer be the dread of the day, but a welcomed force to be reckoned with.

Manifested Purpose

"For this purpose, the Son of God was manifested, that He might destroy the works of the devil." (1John 3:8)

Now we know that the act of God sending His Son into the world was prompted by love.

"God so loved the world..." (John 3:16)

However, it is also very clear, that because of the works of the devil (negative force), the Son of God (positive force) was manifested. Therefore, had there been no devilish works to destroy there would have been no need for the Son of God to appear. It's interesting how the love of God toward humanity is manifested by His desire to destroy the works of the enemy.

The enemy's destruction is not based on the actions of God wiping him from the face of the earth. God empowering His people to trample on serpents and scorpions and to have authority over all the power of the enemy determines his ultimate demise.

Again, it was the demonstrative love and power of God against the forces of darkness that pulled back the curtains of redemption and declared to the world, "Our God reigns!"

Everywhere Jesus went he encountered this positive and negative equation working on the earth. Every time Jesus encountered the "dark side," the kingdom of God visibly increased. From the casting out of spirits, raising the dead, to the calming of the storming seas, the glory, and power of the ***"Word"*** living in the flesh was manifested for all to see. To this day, I am still amazed at how a cross and a tomb, (the extreme opposites) could become the backdrop for resurrection power. (As I mentioned earlier) Take those (two pieces) away and there would have been no revelation of the resurrection power of Jesus Christ.

I remember years back when I signed up for a self-defense class, one of the teachings that stuck out the most was when I was taught to use the weight of my opponent to my advantage. The bigger they were, the bigger the advantage. Of course, this was only true if you knew how to use the techniques of martial arts to counteract the weight rightly.

We have the same advantage in the spirit, the greater the opposition, the greater demonstration of the power of God working in us. We can use the opposing forces of life to our advantage. All we need is the enabling power of God's Spirit to take what the enemy intends for evil and use it for the purposes of God. This is our quest in life, to trust the Father with our lives, never allowing fear and disappointment to seduce us into a place of believing that Jesus has not overcome the world.

Again, I know there are many horrific things going on in our nation and other nations around the world, not to mention in our individual lives, but let me encourage you to stay in faith, continue to believe knowing that nothing, absolutely nothing, can keep you from the loving intentions of God toward you.

"Who shall separate us from the love of Christ?

Shall trouble or hardship or persecution or famine or nakedness or danger or sword?"

"As it is written:

"For your sake we face death all day long; we are considered as sheep to be slaughtered. No, in all these things we are more than conquerors through him who loved us. For I am convinced that neither death nor life, neither angels nor demons, neither the present nor the future, nor any powers, neither height nor depth, nor anything else in all creation, will be able to separate us from the love of God that is in Christ Jesus our Lord." (Rom 8:34-39)

If you enjoyed reading this book, you would also enjoy reading Michael's previous books:

1) Evolution Of Another Kind
2) Space the Prophetic Frontier

You can order these and other products by visiting our website at www.mticenter.com or you can write us at:

Mountain Top International
Po Box 43
Yakima, WA
98907